S0-BFA-942

George Washington

by
Stuart A. Kallen

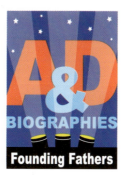

Visit us at
www.abdopub.com

Published by ABDO Publishing Company, 4940 Viking
Drive, Edina, MN 55435. Copyright ©2001 by Abdo
Consulting Group, Inc. International copyrights reserved in
all countries. No part of this book may be reproduced in
any form without written permission from the publisher.

Printed in the United States.

Graphic Design: John Hamilton
Cover Design: MacLean Tuminelly
Cover photo: Corbis
Interior photos:
    American Antiquarian Society, p. 22
    AP/Wide World, p. 5, 7, 8, 39, 40, 47, 50, 51, 59
    Corbis, p. 1, 6, 9, 11, 13, 17, 21, 23, 25, 27, 29, 33, 35,
       41, 43, 45, 49, 53, 56
    John Hamilton, p. 15, 16, 19, 28, 31, 34, 37, 55, 57
    Library of Congress, p. 30
    Mount Vernon Ladies' Association, p. 36

Library of Congress Cataloging-in-Publication Data
Kallen, Stuart A., 1955-
    George Washington / Stuart A. Kallen.
        p. cm. — (The founding fathers)
    Includes index.
    Summary: Presents a biography of the Commander in
Chief of the Continental Army and first president of the United
States.
    ISBN 1-57765-017-4
       1. Washington, George, 1732-1799—Juvenile literature.
2. Presidents—United States—Biography—Juvenile literature.
[1. Washington, George, 1732-1799. 2. Presidents.] I. Title.

E312.66 .K35 2001
973.4'1'092—dc21
[B]
                                98-004806

Contents

Introduction 4

A Simple Beginning 6

Student to Surveyor 8

The Tough Soldier 10

Dangerous Mission 12

Battling the French 14

The Gentleman Farmer 16

A Revolution in the Air 18

The War of Independence 20

A Bloodless Victory 22

Bloody Losses 24

Washington's Daring Plan 26

Valley Forge 28

The War Rages On 32

Final Victory 34

Mount Vernon 36

The Constitutional Convention 38

From Delegate to President 42

Running a Country 44

The Work of the President 46

The Second Term 48

Troubles in the West 52

Back to Mount Vernon 54

Death of a President 56

Conclusion 58

Timeline 60

Where on the Web? 61

Glossary 62

Index 64

Introduction

O N APRIL 30, 1789, cannon shots thundered through the New York City dawn. Instead of causing fear, the noise brought joy to George Washington as he stood before his bedroom mirror. He put white powder in his hair, as was the fashion of the day. He pulled on white silk stockings, a brown suit, and black shoes with silver buckles. He could hear church bells ringing wildly. Finally Washington strapped on his shining steel sword and headed out the door. Excited New Yorkers had gathered in front of Washington's Cherry Street home. A cheer went up when the tall man from Virginia appeared.

Before long the 57-year-old Washington was standing on a balcony overlooking Wall and Broad streets. As thousands of people swarmed below, Washington placed his hand on a Bible. He spoke these words: "I solemnly swear that I will faithfully execute the office of president of the United States and will, to the best of my ability, preserve, protect, and defend the Constitution of the United States."

George Washington takes the oath of office as the first president of the United States.

The buildings shook as the crowd roared. Ships in the harbor fired their guns. Every church bell in the city chimed in. Washington bowed several times and gave a short speech. It was official. The dream of a United States was reality. And President George Washington was to lead this new nation into history.

A Simple Beginning

THE LIFE OF George Washington started in a simple setting. He was born on February 22, 1732, in a plain brick house in Westmoreland County, Virginia. His father was Augustine Washington. His mother was Mary Ball Washington, who was Augustine's second wife. The Washington family was fairly well off. Some of its members had been living in the Virginia colony for 73 years.

When George was six years old, his family settled on a 260-acre (105 hectares) farm called

the Ferry Farm. It was on the Rappahannock River across from Fredericksburg, Virginia. The eight-room house bustled with activity. George had five brothers and three sisters. Two older brothers and one sister were from Augustine's first marriage.

George Washington as a boy cutting down his father's cherry tree. It never really happened.

A recontruction of the 18th century manor house on the farm where George Washington was born on Popes Creek in Westmorland County, Virginia.

While the Washington family farmed tobacco, young George hunted raccoon and deer. He explored the wooded hills on his horse and swam in the clean waters of the Rappahannock. Although the story has been repeated for years, George never chopped down his father's cherry tree.

Student to Surveyor

YOUNG GEORGE began reading, writing, and arithmetic at the age of seven. Arithmetic quickly became his favorite subject. Augustine Washington died when George was 11 years old. Afterwards, George helped run Ferry Farm with his brothers and sisters. George's older half-brother, Lawrence, moved to his own plantation on the Potomac River. While visiting, George met a neighbor named Lord Fairfax, the largest landholder in Virginia. Lord Fairfax taught George how to hunt foxes. He also taught him the manners of a gentleman at dance parties and tea parties.

Lord Fairfax sent a work crew to survey land in the Blue Ridge Mountains. The 16-year-old Washington signed on as an assistant.

A map drawn by George Washington.

Surveyors measure parcels of land for size, shape, and position of boundaries. Washington was very good as a surveyor and before long went into the surveying business. Soon he had earned enough money to buy his own property.

Young George Washington, left, was part of a work crew sent to survey the land holdings of Lord Fairfax in the Blue Ridge Mountains in 1748.

The Tough Soldier

EORGE'S SURVEYING CAREER was halted when his brother Lawrence became ill in the fall of 1751. George took Lawrence, who was stricken with tuberculosis, to the tropical island of Barbados in the West Indies.

The warm sunny climate did little to help Lawrence. Instead, George became sick with small pox. George survived the disease, but his face—especially his nose—was forever scarred by pock marks. Lawrence soon died. The grieving George vowed to follow in his brother's respected footsteps. Since Lawrence had been a member of the colonial army in Virginia, George decided to sign up. At the age of 20, Washington found himself a major in the army.

Facing page: A young George Washington in the colonial army of Virginia.

Dangerous Mission

TROUBLE WAS BREWING in the Ohio River valley. French forts and trading posts were being built on land claimed by the British. And the French were giving rifles to Native Americans, who attacked British fur trappers. Virginia's governor needed a messenger to ride into the wild frontier to tell the French to leave the British territories. Washington volunteered his services.

At 21, Washington stood 6-feet, 2-inches tall. His dark reddish hair and gray-blue eyes impressed his superiors. Soon the young man was leading a party of six men 500 miles into the wilderness. The soldiers crossed rocky mountains, swollen rivers, and icy creeks for 40 days. Washington delivered the message to a large French fort 10 miles south of Lake Erie.

A severe winter storm hampered Washington's return home. When his horse could no longer go on, he continued on foot. When crossing the freezing Allegheny River, Washington slipped from a raft and almost drowned.

Facing page: Major George Washington gives direction to a soldier during his mission to the French commander.

Battling the French

WASHINGTON'S BRAVERY impressed his superiors. He was soon promoted to lieutenant colonel. It was decided that the French must be driven from their forts. Washington re-crossed the Allegheny Mountains with a group of Virginia militiamen. In a battle that was to mark the beginning of the French and Indian War, the troops attacked a company of Frenchmen.

Washington defeated the French and built a fort. But on July 3, 1754, the French fought back, and Washington was forced to surrender the fort. The next year, Washington was chosen to ride with the British army as they attacked the French at Fort Duquesne, where Pittsburgh, Pennsylvania, stands today. The army was caught in the thick forests of Pennsylvania by Indians. Clouds of arrows whizzed through the air and muskets fired at once.

Dozens of British soldiers died trying to escape the ambush. Washington galloped back and forth shouting orders. He later wrote, "I had four bullets through my coat, and two horses shot under me, yet escaped unhurt although death was leveling my companions on every side."

For the next three years, Washington commanded border defenses in Virginia. When the French were finally defeated, Washington gladly resigned from the army. The 26-year-old wrote when he returned home that he found "more happiness in retirement than I ever experienced admidst a wide and bustling World."

Native American forces ambushed George Washington and his troops in the forests of Pennsylvania.

The Gentleman Farmer

GEORGE WASHINGTON married Martha Dandridge Custis on January 6, 1759. She was a widow with two small children who came from a very wealthy family. Washington had been elected to Virginia's governing body, called the House of Burgesses. The family settled down in Williamsburg, where they went to local horse races, theater, and dance balls.

An actor portraying George Washington at Colonial Williamsburg, Virginia.

George Washington at Mount Vernon during a hay harvest.

When lawmaking sessions were over, the Washingtons moved to a farm called Mount Vernon. They used slaves to tend gardens and raise pigs and cows. Mount Vernon was like a small town, with its own blacksmith, leather-making shop, brewery, and tailor shop. Washington called the servants his "family."

A Revolution in the Air

WASHINGTON'S HAPPY days at Mount Vernon were not to last. After the French and Indian War, the British government was searching for a way to pay for the war. The British raised taxes on goods sent to the American colonies. People in the colonies complained loudly.

In 1769, Washington joined with the protesters by refusing to import taxable goods from England. In 1773, a group of men in Massachusetts dressed up like Indians and threw a ship's cargo of tea into Boston Harbor. Washington applauded the "Boston Tea Party." The British enacted strict new laws to punish the colonies. Washington warned that a battle was coming.

In September 1774, delegates of America's 13 colonies gathered to talk about their complaints. Washington represented Virginia in the First Continental Congress at Carpenter's Hall in Philadelphia.

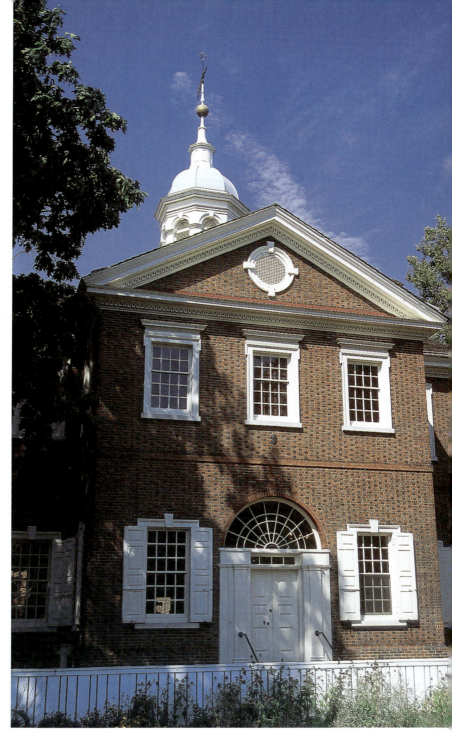

Carpenter's Hall in Philadelphia.

The War of Independence

WASHINGTON HOPED the British would reach a peaceful agreement with the colonies. But on April 19, 1775, the British army, dressed in red coats, fired upon American militia troops in Lexington, Massachusetts. When the smoke cleared, 18 men lay dead or wounded. The "redcoats" pushed on to Concord, looking for weapons and supplies. Boston "minutemen" attacked them from behind trees, walls, fences, and farmhouses. The bloodshed triggered the start of the American Revolution.

In May, Washington attended the Second Continental Congress. Dressed in his military uniform, he quietly announced he was ready to fight. On June 15, 1775, the 43-year-old Washington was unanimously elected general and commander-in-chief of the Continental army.

Within one week, Washington was standing in the middle of a military camp in Boston. The general quickly realized that this was not an army at all. The militiamen often refused to obey orders. Washington wrote that the soldiers were "the most indifferent kind of people I ever saw… and exceedingly dirty and nasty people." But he also wrote, "In little Time we shall work up these raw Materials into good Stuff." During the summer of 1775, Washington drilled the men and gathered supplies.

George Washington takes command of the army at Cambridge, Massachusetts, 1775.

A Bloodless Victory

ON THE NIGHT OF March 4, 1776, Washington's troops dragged 60 cannons onto the hills above Boston's British army camp. When the British soldiers awoke, they saw they had no defense against Washington's army. The British commander exclaimed: "These fellows have done more in one night than I could have made my army do in three months!"

Within days, the redcoats packed up and sailed out of Boston Harbor. Joyful Americans packed the streets in celebration. The Continental army had won its first victory, without shedding any blood. But Washington knew the British would

sail directly for New York City. The general commanded his soldiers to march south and defend the city.

Boston Harbor during the British occupation of the city.

On July 4, 1776, a messenger arrived with the news that the Declaration of Independence had been signed in Philadelphia. The document declared that America was free of British rule. There was no turning back now for Washington. Americans would fight until they were free.

A portrait of George Washington, by Charles Wilson Peale.

Bloody Losses

ON JULY 12, 150 BRITISH ships sailed into New York Harbor. By the next day, 20,000 highly trained British soldiers had landed on Manhattan's beaches. They were joined by 10,000 German troops, called Hessians. Washington's army of 23,000 watched anxiously. By the end of August the fight was on.

On Long Island, Brooklyn Heights, and Manhattan Island, Washington's troops were pounded. Frightened militiamen dropped their guns and ran away. As the weeks wore on, thousands of American troops simply deserted. Those who stayed often lacked such basic supplies as shoes and socks.

But Washington was determined to fight on. In early December, after months of losses, he took his shrunken army across the Delaware River into Pennsylvania. With winter coming on, the redcoats did not follow. Most of the British army returned to the warmth and comfort of New York City. To protect their territory, the British left hundreds of Hessians in outposts across New Jersey.

George Washington prepares for battle.

Washington's Daring Plan

THE BRITISH never thought the rebels would fight back. As Christmas neared, the German soldiers spent their time playing cards and drinking beer, brandy, and wine. While they played, the daring General Washington hatched a plan.

On Christmas Eve 1776, 2,500 American soldiers gathered at McConkey's Ferry on the Delaware River. They got into dozens of boats as a stiff wind beat into their faces. Officer John Fitzgerald later wrote, "It is fearfully cold and raw. A terrible night for the soldiers who have no shoes... but I have not heard one man complain."

Hour after hour the men poled their boats 300 yards (274 m) across the Delaware. After 10 hours the army was ready to march nine miles (14 km) into Trenton, where the Hessians slept. The snow turned to freezing rain, and then back to snow. As the column slipped and stumbled through the dark, Washington urged them to press on.

In this famous painting by Emanuel Gottlieb Leutze, George Washington stands tall as his boat crosses the turbulent water of the Delaware River in 1776.

By dawn the tired army surrounded the village of Trenton. The Hessians were groggy from their Christmas celebrations. Washington's plan had caught them by surprise. In less than two hours 900 German soldiers surrendered. The victory raised the spirits of Washington's small army.

Valley Forge

AFTER TRENTON, Washington plotted several other victories against the British. Using strategy and planning, Washington's troops triumphed against a bigger and stronger force. But the victories would not continue.

By the fall of 1777, the redcoats had conquered Philadelphia. Washington's troops were forced to flee as British soldiers settled in around cozy fires with fine food. The Americans retreated to a hilly camp called Valley Forge, 18 miles (29 km) northwest of Philadelphia.

The Continental soldiers built crude huts from twigs and mud. In a few weeks, thousands of these drafty huts covered the hills. Icy winds blew through the walls. In December, the meat ran out. Men made pasty cakes of flour and water and baked them over hot stones. Washington sent hunters to scour the countryside for food, but they often found nothing.

A cannon stands vigil at Valley Forge National Historic Park in Pennsylvania.

*George Washington meets with the Marquis de
Lafayette at Valley Forge, where the Continental
army suffered through the cold winter of 1777-78.*

George Washington praying at Valley Forge.

If food was bad, clothing was even worse. Dr. Albigence Waldo wrote of a typical soldier's clothes: "His bare feet are seen through his worn-out shoes, his legs nearly naked from the tattered remains of an only pair of stockings, his breeches not sufficient to cover his nakedness, his shirt hanging in strings." The soldiers' feet and legs froze until they turned black. Lice infested their clothes. Disease raged through the camp. Before the cruel winter ended, over 2,000 patriots lay dead. Washington felt pity for his men, but could do nothing to stop their misery.

Although they had suffered terrible hardships during the harsh winter of 1777-78, General Washington's army emerged a toughened fighting force by the following spring.

Conditions improved in February when wagons loaded with meat, grain, and vegetables rolled into camp. Baron von Steuben, a military officer from Prussia, also arrived and taught the men how to fight. In less than a month, the soldiers at Valley Forge were turned into professional soldiers.

The War Rages On

BY APRIL 1778, France had joined with the Americans to fight the British. On a hot day in June, Washington's troops fought the British in New Jersey. After a long battle, the British once again were forced to retreat to New York. The war dragged on for another two years with small victories. The winter of 1780 at Morristown, New Jersey, was as bad as the winter at Valley Forge.

In May 1780, the British began terrorizing the South as they took over Charleston, South Carolina. Worse, Washington discovered that one of his generals, Benedict Arnold, was a traitor.

In 1781, well-trained French soldiers arrived in New York. The professional military men were surprised by Washington's rag-tag army. One French officer wrote, "It is incredible that soldiers composed of men of every age, even of children of fifteen, of whites, blacks, almost naked, unpaid, and rather poorly fed, can march so well and stand fire so steadfastly."

General Washington, on horseback, fights at the Battle of Princeton, New Jersey.

Final Victory

WASHINGTON LEARNED that a large fleet of French ships was sailing to Yorktown, Virginia. A large British force, led by Lord Cornwallis, was also camped at Yorktown. On September 28, Washington's 9,000 troops joined with 7,800 French soldiers on the outskirts of Yorktown.

On October 9, the American and French forces began bombarding Yorktown. French ships blocked the British from escaping to the sea. Dead British and Hessian soldiers lay everywhere. Cornwallis realized his situation was hopeless. On October 17, the British surrendered. Two days later, Cornwallis's soldiers marched out of Yorktown.

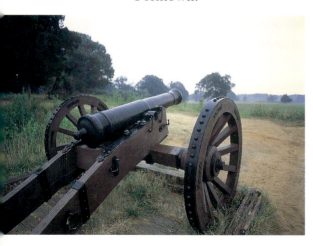

Colonial National Historical Park at Yorktown, Virginia.

General Washington fires the first gun in the bombardment of the British at Yorktown in 1781.

The British surrender at Yorktown was the end of British rule in the colonies. Benjamin Franklin, John Adams, and John Jay met the British in Paris to sign a peace treaty. Washington returned with his army to New York City.

In the fall of 1783, Washington quit the army after eight long, hard years. The last of the British sailed from New York on November 25. On December 4, Washington attended a farewell dinner and eagerly rode back to Mount Vernon in victory.

Mount Vernon

AT THE AGE of 51, George Washington was famous throughout the world. But he happily retired to Mount Vernon, which was suffering from years of neglect. Washington remodeled and repaired his estate. Mount Vernon by now had grown to five separate farms run by 200 slaves.

At home, Washington had so many visitors and well-wishers that it was several years before

Map courtesy Mount Vernon Ladies' Association.

The Mount Vernon estate has changed very little; it looks today much like it did when George Washington owned it over 200 years ago.

The main mansion at Mount Vernon, overlooking the Potomac River.

he and Mrs. Washington ever dined alone. As he aged, Washington lost most of his teeth. Artists painted his picture with his lips clenched tightly together to hide his toothless gums. Eventually, he had false teeth made from hippopotamus tusks.

Even in retirement Washington worried about the new nation. The 13 separate states were run loosely under laws called the Articles of Confederation. There was fighting and bickering between the states, and Washington feared America might fall apart. He believed a new, strong government should be formed to hold the country together.

The Constitutional Convention

WASHINGTON WAS NOT alone in his beliefs. Other politicians, businessmen, and landowners called for a convention to revise the American government. A Constitutional Convention was called in Philadelphia to begin on May 25, 1787.

Washington attended the convention as Virginia's delegate. The other delegates quickly elected the general as their leader.

The summer of 1787 was extremely hot. Day after day, the delegates debated over what form their new government should take. Many supported the vision of James Madison. His ideas called for a strong federal government made up of three branches: legislative (congressmen and senators), executive (the president and his cabinet), and judicial (the courts). Under this system, laws made by the legislature would be carried out by the president. The courts would interpret the laws.

A 1795 oil painting of George Washington by Rembrandt Peal.

On September 17, 1787, Washington joined in with the other delegates in signing the United States Constitution. The document pleased almost no one. There were bitter arguments over its wording. Nine of the 13 states finally voted to ratify the Constitution. Some agreed to the document only if Washington would become the first president. He was the only man they trusted to lead their new nation.

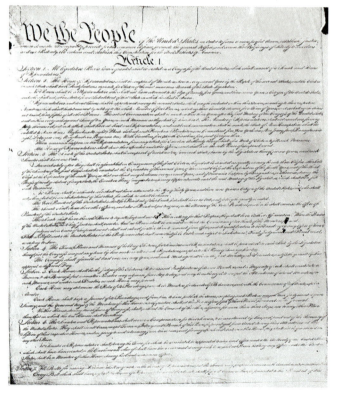

The first page from the United States Constitution.

George Washington watches from his desk as a delegate signs the United States Constitution.

From Delegate to President

WHEN WASHINGTON SIGNED the Constitution, every nation in the world was run by kings, queens, and nobles. No nation in the modern world had ever been ruled by citizens who voted for their leaders. It was a bold experiment and no one—including Washington—knew what the outcome would be.

The new Constitution only allowed land-owning white men to vote. By 1789, two senators and several representatives from each state had been elected. Those men, in turn, elected George Washington as the first president of the United States, in February 1789.

Washington was nervous and did not really want the honor. Expressing his hesitation, he told a friend, "My movements to the chair of government will be like those of a culprit who is going to his execution."

People celebrate in the streets of New York City as George Washington is sworn in as president.

After receiving the official news on April 14, Washington left Mount Vernon for the temporary capital in New York City. By day, cheering crowds lined the roads. At night, Washington was toasted and congratulated in taverns and restaurants. Parades and speeches were given wherever he appeared. On April 30, Washington took the oath of office in Federal Hall.

Running a Country

AS WASHINGTON SETTLED in as first president, he was given 350 clerks and secretaries to help him. He was expected to run the entire country without much more help than he used to run his farm. Washington appointed Alexander Hamilton as the country's first Secretary of the Treasury. Hamilton needed to raise taxes and borrow money from foreign countries to pay off state and national debts.

To persuade southern congressmen to back his tax plan, Washington agreed to build a permanent capital somewhere in the South. The site was located on 10 swampy acres across the Potomac River from Alexandria, Virginia. For the next 10 years streets were designed and buildings constructed in the District of Columbia. In the meantime, the government made its home in Philadelphia.

President George Washington and his Cabinet. From left to right: President Washington; Henry Knox, Secretary of War; Alexander Hamilton, Secretary of the Treasury; Thomas Jefferson, Secretary of State; Edmund Randolph, Attorney General.

Washington picked Thomas Jefferson as Secretary of State. Jefferson had written the Declaration of Independence, and would help Washington with foreign affairs. Although Washington respected both Jefferson and Hamilton, the two men bickered constantly.

The Work of the President

WASHINGTON HAD DOZENS of government posts to fill, from judges to postmaster to ambassadors. Every day office seekers came to him looking for work.

The president appointed John Jay as first Chief Justice of the Supreme Court. Soon after, Congress passed the first 10 amendments to the Constitution that make up the Bill of Rights. These amendments guaranteed Americans basic rights such as free speech, freedom of the press, and freedom of religion.

Washington spent much of his first term traveling across the U.S. Sometimes he visited booming factories in the North. Sometimes he traveled to dusty back-country villages in the deep South. When in Philadelphia, Washington opened the doors to his house every Tuesday afternoon to anyone who wished to visit. On Thursday afternoons, Washington held formal dinners for officials and their families. On Friday evenings, Martha Washington held tea parties.

*Gilbert Stuart's 1796 oil on canvas portrait of
George Washington, on display at the National
Portrait Gallery in Washington D.C.*

The Second Term

ALTHOUGH THE PARTIES offered some relief, Washington soon grew tired of the pressures of the presidency. The battles with Congress and the fights between Jefferson and Hamilton wore him out. As his first term drew to a close in 1793, Washington looked forward to retiring to Mount Vernon. But citizens and politicians alike begged him to run for another term.

Afraid that the fragile country might not hold together, Washington agreed to take another term. Again he was elected by unanimous vote. On March 4, 1793, the 61-year-old president took his second oath of office.

George Washington, painted by Gilbert Stuart.

World events shook the president's calm in Philadelphia. Britain had declared war on France. Many Americans remembered France's help in the American Revolution. They wanted the United States to side with France. But Washington did not want to declare war again on Britain. The United States stayed out of the fight, but Washington's decision made him unpopular for a time.

Actors portraying British troops open fire on a group of French soldiers.

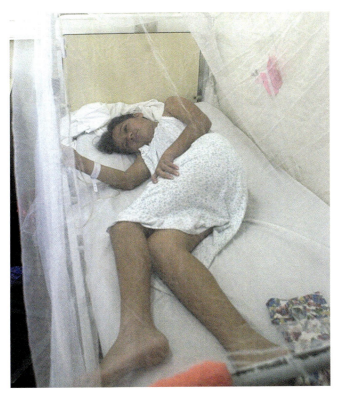

A child suffering from yellow fever. Symptoms of the disease include high fever and chills, severe headache, nausea, vomiting, and diarrhea.

In the summer of 1793, an outbreak of yellow fever threatened the city of Philadelphia. More than 4,000 people got sick and died. Washington led federal workers to nearby Germantown to flee the disease. All business stopped. People poured into the countryside to escape the killer disease. Funeral bells tolled for weeks on end.

Troubles in the West

IN 1794, WARRING INDIANS in Ohio murdered settlers who tried to take their land. Washington sent General Anthony Wayne to defeat the Indians.

Closer to home, western Pennsylvania farmers began an uprising over a new tax on whiskey. Whiskey was the best way the farmers could transport and market the grain they grew. Rather than ship raw grain, it was easier for farmers to turn their corn, barley, and rye into whiskey. Then it was poured into kegs where they could sell it in the East for a dollar a gallon. Taxes of up to 23 cents per gallon were hard for them to bear. To protest, drunken farmers roamed the countryside burning barns. They even tarred and feathered a few tax collectors.

Washington wanted to show the farmers—and the nation—that everyone must obey the federal laws. He tried peaceful measures at first, agreeing to lower the tax. The following week, 5,000 men demonstrated in Pittsburgh. Washington called in militia forces from Pennsylvania, New Jersey, Maryland, and Virginia. Washington rode in to meet the 15,000 militiamen. With such a dazzling show of force, the Whiskey Rebellion was quickly brought to an end.

An angry mob tars a government inspector during the Whiskey Rebellion of 1794.

Back to Mount Vernon

AS WASHINGTON'S second term drew to a close, the new nation was doing very well. Tennessee had joined the United States in 1796. Trade between the states was at an all-time high. American ships sailed to Europe loaded with goods made in the United States. Mills and factories in New England were humming at full production. Cotton was becoming a valuable crop in the South.

Many people hoped Washington would serve as president for life. But in 1796, he published his Farewell Address in a Philadelphia newspaper. He called for peace and justice in America, and he announced his plan to retire. On March 4, 1797, John Adams was elected as the second president of the United States. Washington attended the swearing in and then returned to Mount Vernon.

Washington spent his days in happy retirement. He set about fixing up Mount Vernon again after years of neglect. He rode his horse around his farms. Visitors came and went, and the president answered letters from his admirers.

This statue stands in honor of George Washington in Boston's Public Garden.

Death of a President

I N DECEMBER 1799, the weather at Mount Vernon had turned cold and rainy. But Washington continued his daily rides between the farms. One day he came home wet and shivering. A sore throat began to trouble him. "Let it go as it came," Washington told his

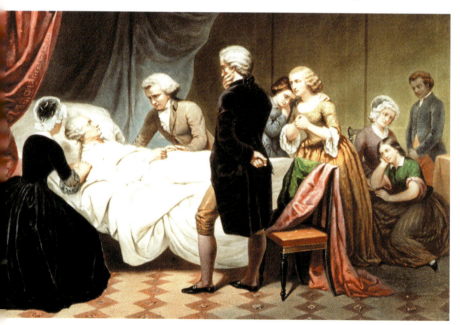

George Washington lies on his death bed while friends come to say their last good-byes.

worried wife. But by the next morning the former president was very sick. Doctors were called.

In those days, doctors believed that draining a patient's blood would help them get better. Doctors decided to "bleed" Washington. They cut his arm with a knife. But the loss of blood further weakened the great man. By the afternoon of December 14, Washington told his secretary "I feel myself going. You had better not take any more trouble about me; but let me go quietly; I cannot last long." With Martha by his side, Washington died around midnight. He was buried four days later at Mount Vernon's family vault.

George Washington's tomb at Mount Vernon.

Conclusion

NEWS OF WASHINGTON'S death quickly spread across the country. The entire nation mourned his passing. Although George Washington never had any children of his own, he was father to an entire nation. In a memorial speech before Congress, Harry Lee praised Washington with these words: "First in war, first in peace, and first in the hearts of his countrymen, George Washington was second to none."

Facing page: The Athenaeum Portrait of George Washington by Gilbert Stuart, 1796. Washington died three years after this portrait was painted.

Timeline

February 22, 1732	George Washington is born in Westmoreland County, Virginia.
1748	Washington becomes a surveyor, working on the lands of Lord Fairfax.
1752	Washington's older brother Lawrence dies. George eventually inherits the Mount Vernon estate.
1754-63	French and Indian War.
1758	Washington returns to Mount Vernon, restoring it from its neglected state.
1759-1774	Serves in Virginia's House of Burgesses.
January 6, 1759	Marries Martha Dandridge Custis.
1774-75	Delegate to the First and Second Continental Congress.
1775-1783	Washington is Congress's unanimous choice as commander in chief of the Continental army during the Revolutionary War.
Summer 1787	Delegate at the Constitutional Convention representing the state of Virginia.
April 30, 1789	Takes office as first president of the United States.
1792	Washington reelected president.
December 14, 1799	Washington dies at his estate at Mount Vernon.

Where on the Web?

The Apotheosis of George Washington
http://xroads.virginia.edu/~CAP/gw/gwmain.html

George Washington
http://sc94.ameslab.gov/TOUR/gwash.html

George Washington's Mount Vernon
http://www.mountvernon.org/

The K-12 Teaching and Learning Center Guide to George Washington
http://tlc.ai.org/washindx.htm

The Papers of George Washington
http://www.virginia.edu/gwpapers/

President George Washington
http://library.thinkquest.org/12587/contents/personalities/gwashington/gw.html

Glossary

American Revolution: the war between Great Britain and its American Colonies that lasted from 1775 to 1783. America won its independence in the war.

Bill of Rights: a statement of the rights of the people that make up the first 10 amendments to the United States Constitution. Some of the amendments guarantee free speech, protection from search and seizure, and the right of a militia to bear arms.

The Colonies: the British territories that made up the first 13 states of the United States. The 13 colonies were the states of New Hampshire, Massachusetts, Rhode Island, Connecticut, New York, New Jersey, Pennsylvania, Delaware, Maryland, Virginia, North Carolina, South Carolina, and Georgia.

Constitution: the document that spells out the principles and laws that govern the United States.

Constitutional Convention: the meeting of men who wrote the United States Constitution.

Continental Army: the army that fought the British in the Revolutionary War.

Continental Congress: the congress that governed the 13 Colonies after they declared their independence from Great Britain.

Declaration of Independence: the document written by Thomas Jefferson that declared America's independence from Great Britain.

House of Representatives: a governing body elected by popular vote to rule a nation.

Militia: a body of citizens enrolled in military service during a time of emergency.

Index

A

Adams, John 35, 54
Alexandria, VA 44
Allegheny Mountains 14
Allegheny River 12
Arnold, Benedict 32
Articles of Confederation 37

B

Barbados 10
Bible 4
Bill of Rights 46
Blue Ridge Mountains 8
Boston, MA 18, 20, 21, 22
Boston Harbor 18, 22
Boston Tea Party 18
Britain 50
British 12, 14, 15, 18, 20, 22, 23, 24, 26, 28, 32, 34, 35
Brooklyn Heights, NY 24

C

Carpenter's Hall 18
Charlestown, South Carolina 32
Cherry Street 4
cherry tree 7
Chief Justice 46
Concord, MA 20
Congress 18, 20, 46, 48, 58
Constitution 4, 38, 40, 42, 46
Continental army 20, 22
Cornwallis, Lord 34
cotton 54

D

Declaration of Independence 23, 45
Delaware 24, 26

Delaware River 24, 26
District of Columbia 44

E

executive branch 38

F

Fairfax, Lord 8
Farewell Address 54
Federal Hall 43
Ferry Farm 6, 8
First Continental Congress 18
Fitzgerald, John 26
Fort Duquesne 14
France 32, 50
Franklin, Benjamin 35
Fredericksburg, VA 6
French 2, 14, 15, 18, 32, 34
French and Indian War 14

G

Germantown, PA 51

H

Hamilton, Alexander 44, 45, 48
Hessian 24, 26, 27, 34
House of Burgesses 16

J

Jay, John 35, 46
Jefferson, Thomas 45, 48
judicial branch 38

L

Lake Erie 12
Lee, Harry 58
legislative branch 38
Lexington, MA 20
Long Island, NY 24

M

Madison, James 38
Manhattan, NY 24
Maryland 53
Massachusetts 18, 20
McConkey's Ferry 26
minutemen 20
Morristown, NJ 32
Mount Vernon 17, 18, 35, 36, 43, 48, 54, 56, 57

N

Native Americans 12
New England 54
New Jersey 24, 32, 53
New York 4, 22, 24, 32, 35, 43
New York City 22, 24, 35, 43
New York Harbor 24

O

Ohio 12, 52

P

Paris, France 35
Pennsylvania 14, 24, 52, 53
Philadelphia, PA 8, 18, 23, 28, 38, 44, 46, 50, 51, 54
Pittsburgh, PA 14, 53
Potomac River 8, 44
Prussia 31

R

Rappahannock River 6, 7

S

Second Continental Congress 20
Secretary of State 45
Secretary of the Treasury 44

slaves 17, 36
small pox 10
South Carolina 32
Supreme Court 46

T

teeth 37
Tennessee 54
Trenton, NJ 26, 27, 28
tuberculosis 10

U

United States 4, 5, 42, 50, 54

V

Valley Forge 28, 31, 32
Virginia 4, 6, 8, 10, 12, 14, 15, 16, 18, 34, 38, 44, 53
von Steuben, Baron 31

W

Waldo, Dr. Albigence 30
Washington, Augustine 6, 8
Washington, Lawrence 8, 10
Washington, Martha Dandridge (Custis) 16, 46, 57
Washington, Mary Ball 6
Wayne, Anthony 5
West Indies 10
Westmoreland County 6
Whiskey Rebellion 53
Williamsburg, VA 16

Y

yellow fever 51
Yorktown, VA 34, 35

STUDY GUIDE AND

PQH467567

SOLUTIONS BOOK FOR

ORGANIC CHEMISTRY:

A SHORT COURSE

HAROLD HART AND

ROBERT D. SCHUETZ

Fourth Edition